PLANT LIFE

Jean F. Blashfield

Science consultant: Suzy Gazlay, M.A., science curriculum resource teacher

Gareth Stevens
Publishing

Please visit our web site at: www.garethstevens.com
For a free color catalog describing Gareth Stevens Publishing's list
of high-quality books, call 1-800-542-2595 (USA)
or 1-800-387-3178 (Canada).

Library of Congress Cataloging-in-Publication Data

Blashfield, Jean F.
    Plant life / Jean Blashfield.
        p. cm. — (Gareth Stevens vital science: life science)
    Includes bibliograpical references and index.
    ISBN-13: 978-0-8368-8442-5 — ISBN-10: 0-8368-8442-6 (lib. bdg.)
    ISBN-13: 978-0-8368-8451-7 — ISBN-10: 0-8368-8451-5 (softcover)
    1. Plants—Juvenile literature.   I. Title.
  QK49.B53   2007
  580—dc22   2007021516

This edition first published in 2008 by
Gareth Stevens Publishing
A Weekly Reader® Company
1 Reader's Digest Road
Pleasantville, NY 10570-7000 USA

Copyright © 2008 by Gareth Stevens, Inc.

Q2a Media editor: Honor Head
Q2a Media design, illustrations and image search: Q2a Media
Q2a Media cover design: Q2a Media

Gareth Stevens art direction: Tammy West
Gareth Stevens graphic designer: Dave Kowalski
Gareth Stevens production: Jessica Yanke
Gareth Stevens science curriculum consultant: Suzy Gazlay, M.A.

Photo credits: t=top, b=bottom, m=middle, l=left, r=right
Photo Researchers, Inc./photolibrary: 5, Science Photo Library/photolibrary: 6, Phototake Inc/
photolibrary: 8, Anastasiya/istock: 11, The Bridgeman Art Library/photolibrary: 15, Science Photo
Library/photolibrary: 16, Botanica/photolibrary: 21, Phototake Inc./photolibrary: 22(t), Phototake
Inc./photolibrary: 22(b), Peter Arnold Images Inc./photolibrary: 24, Yegor Korzh/Shutterstock: 25,
Zastavkin/Shutterstock: 35t, Walter H. Hodge/stillpictures: 35(b), Photo Researchers, Inc./
Photolibrary: 36, Jane Brennecker/iStockphoto: 40(t), Science Photo Library/photolibrary: 40(m),
Animals Animals/Earth Scenes/photolibrary: 40(b), RTimages/Shutterstock: 42, Phototake Inc./
Photolibrary: 43.

Every effort has been made to trace the copyright holders for the photos used in this book.
The publisher apologizes, in advance, for any unintentional omissions and would be pleased
to insert the appropriate acknowledgments in any subsequent edition of this publication.

Printed in the United States of America

 2 3 4 5 6 7 8 9 11 10 09 08 07

Contents

1 What Is a Plant?

Look around you. Unless you are in a school gym or windowless library or basement, you can probably see some green living things. They might be grasses, leafy treetops, a pine tree in winter, a bouquet of roses, even a vast field of wheat or corn growing. All of these living things, or organisms, are plants.

When people were first studying living things, they divided them into two categories, or Kingdoms—plants and animals. They ignored the fact that there were a number of organisms that did not fit well into either category. Some of these organisms are microscopic single-celled bacteria, fungi, such as mushrooms and mold, and red and brown seaweeds.

Today, such oddities are placed in Kingdoms of their own. The Plant Kingdom, called Kingdom Plantae, includes only those organisms with the following characteristics:

• They must be multicellular, made up of more than one cell.

• They must be capable of carrying out photosynthesis, which is the process of plants making their own food— something animals cannot do. The chemicals involved in photosynthesis make plants green.

• In general, they must have roots, stems, and leaves. (There are some exceptions.)

• Finally, according to most botanists, or plant scientists, they must live on land.

This ivy has all the parts of most plants—roots, stems, and leaves.

Being Green

The ways in which plants and animals differ begin at the cells, the microscopic structural "building blocks" of living things. Cells are where the important reactions take place that keep living things moving and growing. Most plant cells contain very special tiny bodies called chloroplasts.

A green chemical called chlorophyll (the prefix "*chloro–*" means "green") works with other chemicals to use the energy in sunlight, carbon dioxide from the air, and water in the cell to make sugar.

Simple sugar, called glucose, is the basic energy storage material for all living things. Every cell in a plant or animal body uses glucose to carry out its functions. Glucose is combined with oxygen to release energy and carbon dioxide. Any glucose not used by the plant right away is stored as a more complex chemical called starch.

Parts of a general plant cell. Not all cells have all parts.

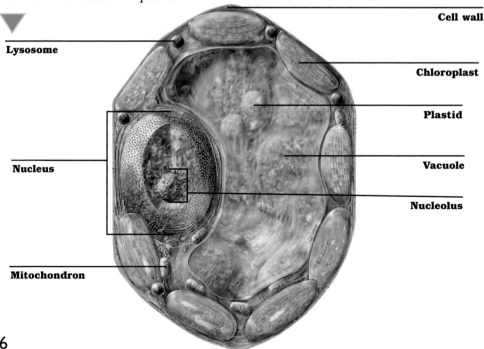

Cell wall

Lysosome

Chloroplast

Plastid

Nucleus

Vacuole

Nucleolus

Mitochondron

6

The reaction that allows plants to make their own food is simple:

carbon dioxide + water + sunlight —> glucose + oxygen

Chemically, this is written:

$$6\ CO_2 + 6\ H_2O + \text{sunlight} \longrightarrow C_6H_{12}O_6 + 6\ O_2$$

In addition to chloroplasts, plant cells also contain (as do animal cells) other tiny bodies called mitochondria. Mitochondria use oxygen to burn carbon compounds (glucose) for energy in the process called respiration. This is when a plant takes in gases from the atmosphere and expels gases, such as

Cell Walls

All cells have a cell membrane around them, which separates one cell from another. But most plant cells have an additional cell wall that protects the contents of the cell. It is made of cellulose, a tough material constructed of complex chemicals called carbohydrates. Paper is made primarily of cellulose from trees. Cotton fiber is almost pure cellulose. Environmentalists talk about using biomass (material of biological origin) as a source of energy to replace oil. The main source of biomass is cellulose in plant matter.

oxygen, into the air. Animals also carry out respiration, of course, but plants use a lot less oxygen in respiration than animals do. This is why plants evolved on Earth first and helped oxygen to build up in the atmosphere. When enough oxygen was established in Earth's atmosphere, animals could start to evolve. Today, oxygen makes up about one-fifth of our atmosphere.

The Problem of Water

Land is a much more hospitable place for plants than the seas and oceans. More sunlight is available and the gases needed for life flow freely in the atmosphere. The problem plants face, though, is how to get and retain the water they need. Water is vital because about 90 percent of a plant is water. Much of the variety found in plants has to do with the ways they have adapted to solve the problem of getting and keeping water.

The first solution for land plants was to protect what water is in them already. To do this, they developed a waxy substance called the cuticle that covers most of

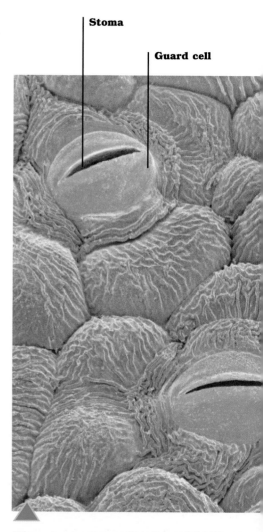

Stoma

Guard cell

The stoma in a plant's epidermis can open or close.

the plant's exposed surfaces. The cuticle is not cellular. It is produced by the outer layer of cells, called the epidermis. Its job is to prevent water and gases from escaping from the interior of the plant.

In preventing water and gases from escaping, however, the cuticle also keeps water and gases from entering the plant. The solution to this problem was for the plant to develop holes in the surface of its leaves and sometimes on its stems. These holes are called stomata (singular *stoma*). They are made by guard cells that can open or close, depending on the plant's needs. Most stomata are on the undersides of the leaves.

When the stomata open, carbon dioxide enters the leaf and extra oxygen exits. Water can also enter or exit through the stomata. Water evaporating through the stomata is a process called transpiration.

The Cacti

Plants that can actually store water are often found in deserts. Cacti are the most famous plants for doing this. The stem of a cactus is plump and its cuticle is thick because it must hold water. Cacti do not have leaves because leaves give up too much moisture. Instead, they have sharp spines, which both protect it from animals and create a sunshade that limits the amount of sun reaching the surface of the plant. A cactus's stomata close during the day and open at night, which is the reverse of most plants.

Staying in Place

The more primitive plants do not have real roots. They just have little hairs that anchor them in place. Higher plants, however, have true roots that also absorb water and minerals from the soil.

9

There are two main kinds of roots. A taproot is a single thick root that grows down from the stem. It usually has some smaller rootlets that branch out from it. A carrot is a taproot.

A fibrous root system has many small roots that reach out widely from the plant stem. Grasses have fibrous roots that tangle together in the soil.

Both kinds of roots have fine root hairs on their outside surfaces. Water enters the system through the root hairs. It carries minerals the plant needs, such as phosphorus, potassium, and nitrogen.

Not everything that grows underground is a root. Some plants have stems that grow horizontally underground. New plants grow upward from these stems. This method is a type of asexual reproduction. These underground stems are called rhizomes. Lilly of the valley plants spread by rhizomes. Above the ground,

similar horizontal stems are called stolons. Strawberries spread by stolons.

Though plants stay in place, anchored by roots, parts of the plant may move in response to something outside the plant. These movements are called tropisms. They may be in response to light, including sunlight (phototropism), water (hydrotropism), or even gravity (gravitropism). Roots grow downward because of gravity. Stems grow upward because of light.

Leaf Structure

A leaf is usually a flat expanse of cells. Leaves are generally green because they contain chorophyll. Most photosynthesis occurs in leaves, but it also occurs in stems. The outer leaf surface is cuticle, which is produced by the epidermis cells. Sunlight goes through cuticle and epidermis to strike the chloroplasts where the plant's

Part of the diversity found in plants comes from the shapes of both simple and compound leaves.

food is produced. Some leaves are even simpler. The leaves on mosses are only one layer of cells thick.

Individual kinds of plants are usually recognizable by their leaf shape. Each shape and arrangement of leaves evolved in response to the needs of the plant. Usually this has to do with obtaining the right amount of sunlight. A leaf usually has a stalk attaching it to the plant stem. A leaf can turn on its stalk, in response to wind or sunlight, without breaking.

In general, there are two main kinds of leaves: simple and compound. A simple leaf consists of a single blade. A maple leaf is a simple leaf. A compound leaf consists

11

The Panda's Thumb

As plants and animals evolved, some specific animals developed both behavior and physical adaptations in response to specific plants. For example, the giant panda of China eats only the young leaves from bamboo plants. The panda's relationship to bamboo is so important that it evolved an extra-long wrist bone that can be used as a "thumb." The panda uses this "thumb" to grasp bamboo stems while it nibbles the tender leaves. Other related animals do not have such an adaptation. In fact, the panda's closest relatives—bears and raccoons—eat other plants and meat. Pandas get little nutrition from bamboo leaves. Their bodies cannot store food, so they do not hibernate as their meat-eating relatives do.

of several small leaflets arranged on a stalk. Clover and rose bushes have compound leaves.

All leaves have some veins in them. The veins carry water and sugars. The largest one, at the center of a leaf, extends from the stalk. It is the midrib, a vein that gives the leaf strength. We will learn more about veins, part of the vascular system, in later chapters.

Circle of Life

Plants and animals must exist together. Only plants can make their own food. Animals have to eat plants (or animals that have eaten plants) to obtain the food they need to carry on the functions of life. Together, plants and animals form a circle of life. Energy flows first from plants, then to animals that eat plants. Animals release their droppings, which break down in soil. Energy flows back to plants that grow in this soil.

Herbivores are animals that eat strictly plant material. Their digestive systems can handle the tough cellulose in plant matter. They do not absorb cellulose, however, so their digestive systems must get all their nutrients from the other material in the plant matter as efficiently as possible.

Cattle and other bovines have extra stomachs to digest tough plant matter. In one of these stomachs the plant matter is fermented by bacteria into a more digestible form.

🔑 Pronunciation Key:

alga (AL-guh)

algae (AL-jee)

biome (BY-ohm)

cuticle (KEW-tih-kul)

herbivore (ER-bih-vor)

mitochondria
(my-toh-KAHN-dree-uh)

stoma (STO-muh)

stomata (STO-mah-tuh)

vascular (VASS-kew-luhr)

Plants Creating Biomes

A biome is the largest category of natural habitat, taking in all the similar habitats around the world. A biome is often named after the plant life it features. For example, grasslands feature grasses. Although various individual grasslands are scattered around the planet, all of them are part of the grassland biome. Both North American prairies and tropical grasslands, called savannas, are included in the grassland biome. Biomes are determined by the climate, too. All the tropical rain forests throughout the world, for example, are part of the tropical rain forest biome. Other biomes include tundra, desert and semi-desert, conifer forest, temperate deciduous forest, and temperate rain forest.

2 How Plants Are Classified

Changing Names

Until recently, there was little consistency in how plant categories were named. Now, most botanists follow the rules established by The International Code of Botanical Nomenclature (ICBN). This code was adopted by the International Botanical Congress to establish firm rules for classification and for giving names to newly discovered plants.

Carl von Linné was a Swedish scientist and physician, born in 1707. He developed a way to group and name plants and animals so that people all over the world could be sure they were talking about the same organism. He gave each plant or animal a two-part Latin name. The first part is the Genus (plural: Genera). The second part is the Species. Linné himself took a two-part Latin name—he became Carolus Linnaeus.

Linnaeus looked around him and divided the living things he saw into two great Kingdoms. These Kingdoms were plants and animals. The animals moved around and the plants generally did not. The plants were also mostly green.

Carolus Linnaeus, the eighteenth-century naturalist who developed the binomial, or two-name, system of naming living things

What Is a Species?

Botanists study plants and look for new Species.

A Species is a group of plants or animals capable of breeding with each other but with no other similar plants or animals. They are named within Linnaeus's two-word term, Genus and Species. (The Species name is never used alone.) This definition does not work with some organisms, however. Some plants reproduce asexually. Also, some plants can be fertilized by a similar plant from another species.

For many generations, scientists were content to follow Linnaeus's guidance, though they knew that some things just did not fit very well into either Kingdom. Fungi do not fit either Kingdom. They do not move around, but they are not green. Linnaeus decided, however, to put them with plants. He knew nothing about bacteria or cells.

Antonie van Leeuwenhoek of Holland (1632–1723) had already discovered living things that did not fit well into Linnaeus's Kingdoms. When Leeuwenhoek discovered incredibly tiny creatures through the lens of his newly invented microscope, he called them "animalcules."

New Kingdoms

The microscope opened up the world of the very small. Biologists could see both one-celled creatures as well as actual cells from which larger plants and animals were made. These cells sometimes looked much like the one-celled creatures. Biologists began to consider ways of arranging living things into categories based on characteristics seen only with a microscope.

The first new Kingdom added was *Protista*. German scientist Ernst Haeckel (1834–1919) suggested that Leeuwenhoek's "animalcules" should have a category of their own, one made up of single-celled creatures. He included as protists both single-celled animals, such as amoebas, and single-celled plants, such as certain algae.

Later, scientists saw that there were really two very distinct groups within Haeckel's protists. One group had cells with a nucleus, or central body containing genetic material. This group is now called the eucaryotes, which means "true nucleus." The others, without a nucleus, are call procaryotes, meaning "before nucleus."

Toward the end of the twentieth century, scientists developed the ability to study the molecules within cells. This study finally led to the classification system in use in the twenty-first century.

Why Classify?

The science of classifying living things is called taxonomy. A taxonomic group, or category, is called a taxon (plural: *taxa*). But why bother? Isn't classifying plants just like putting things in a large filing cabinet? How important can that be?

First, let's look at Linnaeus's Latin names. Their use simplifies communication. If botanists, gardeners, and farmers all over the world use the same name for a plant, they know they are talking about exactly the same plant.

The dandelion is called different things in different places. In addition to dandelion, it may be known as the blowball or faceclock.

But anyone interested knows exactly which plant is being discussed if it is called by its Latin name, *Taraxacum officinale*. The first part of the name is the Genus, which is always capitalized, and the second part is the Species, which always starts with a lowercase letter.

A number of Genera with similar characteristics are put into a larger category, a Family. Then a number of Families may be grouped together in an even larger category, an Order, and so on, up to the largest category, Kingdom Plantae.

Classification is always changing. The most recent big change came with the study of the genes that determine what each plant will be. Genetics, the study of genes, has allowed botanists to discover previously unknown connections between plants. The classification of plants is an ongoing process.

Divisions

Botanists use the term Division for one of the largest categories of plants. This is the same category that a zoologist calls a Phylum. A simple classification of the twelve Divisions of plants can be made.

Divisions are divided into Classes. In the boxed listing (right), angiosperms and gymnosperms are Classes. Angiosperms are divided into two Subclasses, dicots and monocots. The next important category is the Family. Some botanists, however, put Orders and Super-orders between the Subclasses and Families.

Categories have specific endings to their names. Order names, for example, end in *–ales* and Family names end in *–aceae*.

⚿ Pronunciation Key:

fungi (*FUHN-jee*) or (*FUHN-gee*)
Genera (*JEH-nay-ruh*)
genetic (*juh-NEH-tik*)
Genus (*JEE-nuss*)

Primitive plants	Bryophytes		Reproduce by spores (3 Divisions)
Vascular plants	Primitive vascular plants		Reproduce by spores (4 Divisions)
	Higher vascular plants		Reproduce by seeds
		Gymnosperms	No flowers (4 Divisions)
		Angiosperms	Flowering plants (1 huge Division)
		Monocots	Single seed leaf, leaves with parallel veins
		Dicots	Double seed leaf, leaves with netted veins

An Example of Classification

This is the full classification of the common dandelion:

Kingdom	*Plantae* – plants
Subkingdom	*Tracheobionta* – vascular plants
Superdivision	*Spermatophyta* – seed plants
Division	*Magnoliophyta* – flowering plants
Class	*Magnoliopsida* – dicotyledons
Subclass	*Asteridae*
Order	*Asterales*
Family	*Asteraceae* – aster
Genus	*Taraxacum* – dandelion
Species	*Taraxacum officinale* – common dandelion

3 Primitive Land Plants

The simplest land plants include mosses, liverworts, and hornworts. They may be all around you, especially mosses, but you may not notice them. These primitive plants are called bryophytes, though only true mosses belong to the Division called *Bryophyta*. Botanists used to put all three kinds of bryophytes in one Division, but more recently they have found that mosses, liverworts, and hornworts all evolved from different ancestors.

Like fungi and algae, bryophytes reproduce by spores, which are small bodies capable of growing into new organisms. Spores originally grew on the tips of primitive plant stalks. Later, they sometimes grew on the backs of leaves. Spores have

Coming Back to Life

One clubmoss relative, called *Selaginella*, can survive drought. It lives in the deserts of the Southwest United States and Central America. In a drought, it dries up into a tight little ball and goes dormant. When rain falls, it turns green again.

hard coverings that prevent them from drying out until they are dispersed, or spread through the environment by wind or water. When they settle into soil, spores grow into new plants exactly like their parent plants. Clubmosses, ferns, and horsetails are not bryophytes. They are more highly evolved organisms, but they also reproduce by spores.

Badge moss is one of many bryophytic plants that reproduce by spores.

Simple Reproduction

Most reproduction, for both plants and animals, is sexual. That means that an egg from the female combines with a sperm from the male to produce a new organism, an embryo. The egg and sperm each contribute one set of the genetic material called chromosomes, giving the embryo characteristics from each parent. Sexual reproduction results in the great diversity of plants and animals found on Earth today.

All cells must multiply to keep organisms growing and to replace worn-out cells. Most cells divide by all parts of them doubling. Then the resulting extra-big cell splits. That kind of "multiplication by division" is called mitosis.

When reproductive cells, called gametes, divide, they must end up with only one set of chromosomes. The cell division process that accomplishes this is called meiosis. Once the male and female gametes have combined, the resulting cell has the needed number of genes. After that, the organism grows as the cells multiply via mitosis without a change in the number of genes.

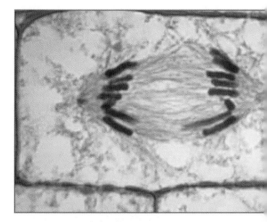

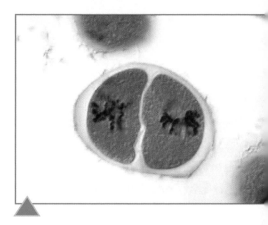

In mitotic cell division (top), chromosomes separate before the cytoplasm divides into two cells. Meiotic cell division (bottom), produces cells with half the chromosomes.

22

Alternation of Generations

The spores of bryophytes contain only one set of chromosomes, a condition called haploid. Plants that grow from haploid spores are called gametophytes.

How can a plant survive with only one-half the required number of chromosomes? It relies on a trait called alternation of generations. Most plants, even the seed plants we see around us, undergo a type of alternation of generations. This process evolved when some plants developed spores that grew in two varieties, one small, called microspores, and one larger, called megaspores. These gradually evolved into male and female parts, starting sexual reproduction.

The green, carpet-like mass formed by mosses, for example, is made up of adult plants. A single moss plant, or gametophyte, puts out two structures. One, called the archegonium, produces eggs. The other structure, the antheridia, produces sperm. Both eggs and sperm are haploid, with only one set of chromosomes. When they link up in the watery environment that mosses require, they form the next generation, called sporophytes. Sporophytes are diploid; they contain two sets of chromosomes. They form swollen structures called capsules, containing, as a result of meiosis, new haploid spores. When the new spores are dispersed, they grow into more gametophytes. Thus the sporophytes and gametophytes are alternate phases, or generations, of true mosses.

Bryophyte Characteristics

An important characteristic of mosses, hornworts, and liverworts is that they are the only land plants in which the gametophyte generation is the one seen. As we will see later, most other plants also have an alternation of generations, but the familiar plant we recognize is the sporophyte. The gametophyte generation may have been reduced to no more than a few specialized cells.

Another characteristic of bryophytes is that they do not have roots to hold them to the ground. Instead, they have hairlike structures called rhizoids. Rhizoids consist of rows of cells attached to each other in strings. Unlike roots, they do not absorb water, they just anchor the plant to the surface on which it is growing.

Though mosses are usually so small that you cannot distinguish the parts, they have stems and leaves. The leaves may have a midrib, just like the leaves on trees. The leaves generally grow in a spiral around the stem. Not all mosses spread out flat. One moss found on the moist floors of the temperate rain forest in New Zealand may reach 2 feet (60 centimeters) high.

The "Worts"

Liverworts and hornworts are the most primitive of the bryophytes. The suffix "wort" is from the Old English word for "plant."

There are about six thousand Species of liverworts, which belong to Division *Hepaticophyta.* They are the simplest of true plants. Their gametophyte generation looks like a flat leafy structure, which you may see lying on rocks in shady places. The leafy part, called a thallus, has pores on the surface, but

The flat "leaf" of this liverwort is the thallus. The umbrella-like structures are the male and female parts.

24

they are not true stomata. Liverworts are so primitive that they do not even have a cuticle to prevent them from drying out. If a piece of the thallus breaks off and lands in moist soil, it can grow into a new plant. This method of reproduction is very primitive. Liverworts also reproduce sexually.

Hornworts (Division *Anthocerophyta*) are scarce—there are only about one hundred Species. They get their name from the fact that the thallus may send out tall, hornlike structures. They are the sporophyte generation.

True Mosses

The main bryophytes are true mosses (Division *Bryophyta*). There are almost ten thousand Species found all over the world. Mosses generally have leaves that are only one cell thick. They soak up water from their environment.

Even though mosses are bryophytes, they have the beginnings of a water-

Water-Holding Moss

Sphagnum moss can absorb a huge amount of water.

Sphagnum moss, also called peat moss, is a Family of true mosses with the amazing ability to soak up as much as twenty times their own weight in water. As peat moss grows, new cells form around dead cells. The dead cells make pockets that hold water. For this reason, peat moss is often mixed with soil to increase the water-holding capacity for house or garden plants. This same moss is one of the makers of peat and coal, a fuel.

25

transporting system. They have specialized cells that link up to form strands, which can carry water and nutrients through the plant. These specialized cells are not enough, though, to allow mosses to grow large. Size takes bigger, stronger fluid-carrying vessels. Such vessels are called tracheids, and the plants that have them are called tracheophytes.

A New Vascular System

Every plant that is not a bryophyte is a tracheophyte. It has special veins—the vascular system—that carry water through the plant. The veins consist of two kinds of tubes combined into what are called vascular bundles. One kind of tube is xylem, a word that comes from the Greek for "wood." Xylem cells, which are dead, are made of strong but flexible cellulose. Flowers are the only part of a plant that do not contain xylem.

Xylem functions somewhat like a straw in your glass. When you suck on the top of the straw, the liquid rises. In a plant, no one is sucking on the top of the xylem vessel, but water is evaporating from the leaves at the top of the plant. That evaporation, called transpiration, creates a suction that makes the water rise, carrying minerals with it.

Surrounding the tubes of xylem are tubes called **phloem,** which is from the Greek for "bark." The phloem carries the sugar made by photosynthesis in the leaves down the stem and distributes it to the other parts of the plant. The sugar is in the form of sap, which is needed for energy and growth by those plant parts that do not make their own food, such as roots and flowers.

Between the xylem and phloem tubes is the plant's cambium. This cambium is the layer of cells that produces both the xylem and the phloem. The development of new xylem tubes during the growth period each year produces the annual rings visible in a cross-section of a tree trunk. Until a tree is cut, the vascular bundles in the trunk are not visible, but they show in leaves of all higher plants as veins.

All parts of a plant, from root to leaf tip, are provided with water by a network of tubes called the vascular system.

The Most Primitive Vascular Plants

Clubmosses, also called lycopods (Division *Lycophyta*), are the most primitive of the vascular plants. They were among the earliest plants to inhabit the land. As they developed, they were able to occupy drier regions and grow taller. In the Carboniferous Era (more than 300 million years

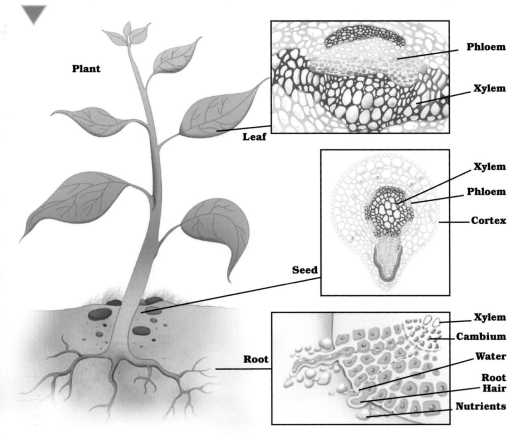

Plant

Leaf

Phloem

Xylem

Xylem

Phloem

Cortex

Seed

Root

Xylem

Cambium

Water

Root Hair

Nutrients

ago), many of the trees that eventually formed coal were lycopods that grew to be 80 to 100 feet (24 to 30 meters) high.

The mosslike form of clubmoss is the sporophyte generation, while true mosses show up as the gametophyte generation. In temperate regions, clubmosses grow on the ground. In the tropics, they are often epiphytes, which means they grow on trees.

Horsetails (Division *Sphenophyta*) grew in ancient times as tall trees, especially trees called calamites. They contributed to the deposits of coal we mine today. The only horsetail Genus found today is *Equisetum*. These plants look like miniature conifers. The "branches" grow in whorls around the stem.

The Dominant Ferns

Ferns (Division *Pterophyta*) make up the largest group of non-flowering plants. There are probably 11,000 Species found throughout the world. They are the most complex of the plants that do not produce seeds.

We think of ferns as having lots of feathery divided leaflets on long stems, or fronds, like the common ferns found in moist woods. Not all ferns are like that, however. Many have large single leaves, and some are even treelike, though they do not form permanent woody tissue. They may reach 40 to 50 feet (12 to 15 m) high.

🔑 Pronunciation Key:

antheridia (*AN-thuh-RIH-dee-uh*)

archegonium (*AR-kee-GO-nee-um*)

bryophyte (*BRY-uh-fyt*)

chromosome (*KROHM-oh-sohm*)

gamete (*GAM-eet*)

gametophyte (*guh-MEE-tuh-fyt*)

meiosis (*my-OH-siss*)

mitosis (*my-TOH-siss*)

phloem (*FLOW-uhm*)

rhizoid (*RYE-zoyd*)

sporophyte (*SPOR-uh-fyt*)

tracheid (*TRAY-kee-uhd*)

xylem (*ZY-luhm*)

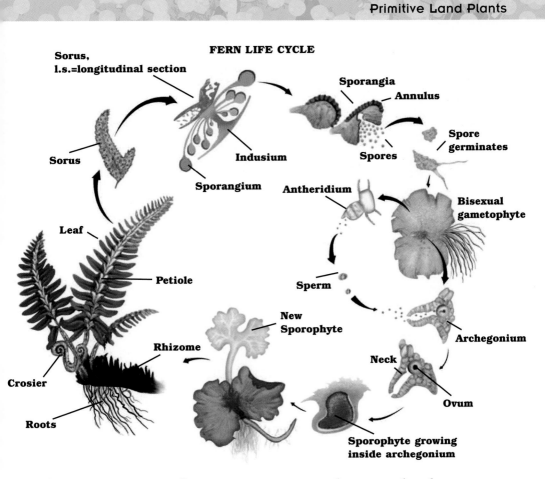

FERN LIFE CYCLE

Sorus, l.s.=longitudinal section

Sorus

Leaf

Petiole

Crosier

Roots

Rhizome

Sporangium

Indusium

Sporangia

Annulus

Spores

Spore germinates

Antheridium

Bisexual gametophyte

Sperm

New Sporophyte

Neck

Archegonium

Ovum

Sporophyte growing inside archegonium

The most common fern Order is *Filicales*. The pretty long fronds are the sporophyte generation. They produce spores that grow in tiny but plentiful cases, called sori, visible on the back of the leaves. When the spores drop to the ground, they develop into gametophytes that are so small they are almost invisible on the soil. In the damp soil, eggs and sperm develop, separately. The sperm fertilize the eggs, and a new generation of sporophytes begins to grow.

Ferns also reproduce by rhizomes—stems that spread horizontally under the ground. New shoots of the sporophyte generation grow upward from the rhizomes. They are visible in the spring as little curls called fiddleheads, or crosiers.

4 Seeds and Flowers

Plants with a vascular system to transport water and sugars can develop parts with different functions—leaves, roots, stems, and finally seeds and flowers. Plants that produce seeds are called spermatophytes. These are the plants that have determined the look and shape of much of our landscape. Seed plants became dominant about the time that dinosaurs did, during the Mesozoic Era, about 200 million years ago.

Seed plants are generally divided into two groups, gymnosperms, which do not have flowers, and angiosperms, which do. The angiosperms, or flowering plants, are all in one Division, *Magnoliophyta* (also called *Anthophyta*). There may

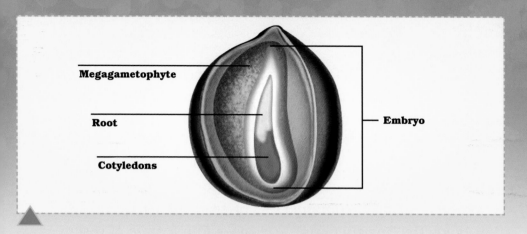

Gymnosperm

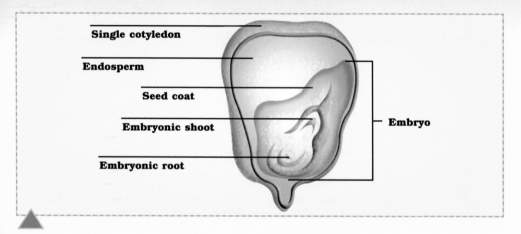

Monocotyledon (Angiosperm)

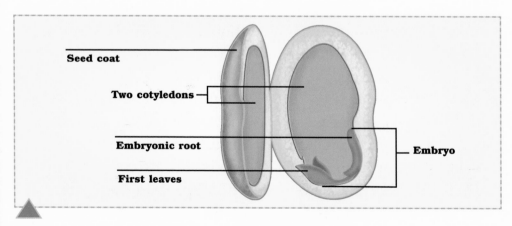

Diocotyledon (Angiosperm)

be as many as 260,000 Species of flowering plants that we know about with many more still to be discovered.

What Is a Seed?

A seed is basically a container that holds the "instructions" for how to build a plant. Seeds do not exist until a female egg has been fertilized by male sperm. Then the egg container, or ovule, develops into a seed. A seed consists of many cells. Each seed contains a single tiny plant, called an embryo, that grows into the adult plant.

Male and female cells developed from spores. Small spores (microspores) evolved into male pollen grains, which are covered by a tough coating that keeps them from drying out. The larger spores (megaspores) turned into female sex cells, or eggs, which are located in ovules.

When a pollen grain reaches a female plant part, it grows a tube. Plant sperm travels along this tube into the ovule. There,

the sperm fertilizes the egg, making an embryo. The ovule then matures into a seed and accumulates a food layer called the endosperm. The ovule develops a protective covering, or seed coat. The embryo goes into a state of rest until conditions of moisture, warmth, oxygen, and light are right for it to start growing, or to germinate. That may be days or it may be many years, but as soon as water is absorbed, the embryo can begin to grow. A tiny part emerges through the seed coat and becomes the first roots. A new plant is growing, using the endosperm for its first food.

Seeds can vary greatly, even though they do the same job. A coconut as large as a bowling ball is the seed of the coconut palm tree. It has a thick husk that enables it to float long distances across the ocean. Seeds can also be very tiny. The little, dark-blue poppy seeds often used on bagels are the seeds of poppy plants.

Seed Dispersal

One of the most interesting things about seeds is how they get spread around, or dispersed. Some of them are so lightweight they can be blown by the wind. Dandelions, for example, usually grow in open areas. When they mature, their yellow flower head turns to white fluff, which is attached to the seeds. Wind or the puff of a person's breath scatters, or disperses, the seeds. Maple trees have their seeds encased in a flat blade that can spin in the wind like a helicopter blade.

Angiosperms all develop fruit, which are ripened ovaries. Many fruits are not noticeable. Others, such as apples, oranges, and bananas,

are important food crops. Nuts, tomatoes, and squash are all fruits, too. Basically, fruit is formed as a method for dispersing seeds.

Some fruits depend on animals to disperse them. Brightly colored berries contain seeds that many birds eat. The seeds remain intact during digestion because of their tough seed coats. They are deposited in soil with the birds' droppings. Some seeds have hooks on them that catch in the fur of passing mammals. The animals may carry such burrs long distances before they fall off. Various thistles spread in that way.

Some seeds need nothing more than gravity to disperse them. The seeds in a mature apple, for example, are released when the ripe fruit falls to the ground. The fruit rots where it falls, and the seeds may be able to sprout. Beneath the parent tree, however, is not a good place for new plants to germinate.

Pronunciation Key:

boreal (*BOR-ee-uhl*)
coniferous (*kuh-NIH-fuh-ruhss*)
gnetophytes (*nee-TUH-fyt*)
spermatophyte
(*spur-MAH-tuh-fyt*)

They are blocked from both sunshine and rain.

Gymnosperms

The oldest category of seed plants is the gymnosperm, which means "naked seed." The seeds are not enclosed in an ovary. Instead, they lie exposed on the scales of a cone or similar structure.

All gymnosperms used to be included in one Division. Now, though, botanists see that they evolved from four different ancestors. They are cycads, ginkgoes, conifers, and a small group called gnetophytes (Division *Gnetophyta*). One type of gnetophyte produces ephedra, a drug that was, until recently, used in decongestant medicines.

The cycads (Division *Cycadophyta*) include plants called sago palms, but they are not palms. Instead, they are what remains of an ancient group of plants that would have been a common food source for dinosaurs.

Some of them look like pineapples. All of them have leaves arranged in a bunch that spreads from the top of a fat stem. Cycads are primarily tropical, but many have been brought to northern lands as decorative outdoor plants.

The ginkgo, or maidenhair tree, is the only plant in the *Ginkgophyta* Division. The tree's fan-shaped leaves are common sights in parks. It can produce many fruits, however, that turn into foul-smelling mush where they fall. The leaves are shed in the fall. The gingko is usually placed in its own Division because its reproduction is partly like the cycads and partly like the conifers.

Conifers

Like the cycads and ginkgo, conifers (Division *Pinophyta* or the older name *Coniferophyta*) are gymnosperms. There are far fewer Species of conifers than there are Species of

Two gymnosperm Divisions: conifer (top) and cycad (bottom).

colder temperatures than angiosperms can.

Conifers are named after their reproductive structure, which is a cone. Most trees bear both small male and large female cones. The male cones have pollen within their scales. When the cones open, the pollen can float with the wind, landing on the cones of the same tree or one nearby. Young female cones lie slightly open, so the pollen can land between the scales, where ovules lie.

When ovules have been fertilized, the scales close up and the embryonic plants mature for up to three years. When the seed cones open again, the mature seeds can drop to the ground, to start a new generation. The trees that grow are the sporophyte generation. The gametophyte generation has almost disappeared.

Some conifers have cones that never open to release

trees that flower, but conifers have created vast areas of forest throughout the northern world. Coniferous forests are often called boreal forests, meaning "northern." They can tolerate much

35

seeds unless fire endangers the parent tree. The heat makes the cones open and the seeds are ready to grow in burned ground.

Most conifers have needle-like leaves that are evergreen and stay on the tree for many years, though they are gradually replaced. The leaves in the cypress Family, however, are scale-like, and the needles of the larch Family are deciduous, meaning they

When scales on the cone of a conifer open up, seeds can drop to the ground.

fall off each autumn. Not all conifer cones are woody. Some are fleshy, and the yew Family produces red fleshy cup-shaped fruit-like structures instead of cones. Most conifers grow in the north.

Angiosperms

The largest group of plants is the angiosperms, the flowering plants, belonging to Division *Anthophyta*. They have certainly not all been identified yet, but at least 260,000 Species are known. Unless you live in a dense pine forest, most of the plants you see around you are angiosperms.

The name angiosperm, meaning "covered seed," is based on *angeion*, which means "vessel." The vessel refers to the ovary, in which the female sex cell, or ovule, lies. Angiosperms are much more diverse than conifers, primarily because of their vessels. They can be tiny flowers, lost among grass on a lawn, or they can be giant trees. The world's largest flower is called *Rafflesia arnoldii*, a native of Sumatra. Its red, polka-dotted blossom may be a 39 inches (100 cm) across.

The ovule is part of a set of structures that are the female parts of the flower. The whole set is called the carpel. It includes the ovule inside an ovary, with an elongated part, the style, rising above it. The top of the style is enlarged as the stigma. The stigma is usually sticky to make any pollen coming its way stick to it. The male parts of a flower are the stamens, which consist of an anther, which bears the pollen, rising out of the filament.

Both male and female parts are inside the more colorful flower parts. On many flowers, the most obvious parts are the petals. They attract insects to the flower. The sepals, located outside the petals, may be green or another color.

The most efficient pollination occurs through the movement of insects. They brush against the pollen, catching some on the tiny hairs on their bodies. Then, when they enter another flower, the pollen may be caught by the sticky surface of the stigma. The pollen then develops a tiny pipe, the pollen tube, which grows down through the style until it reaches the ovule. There it fertilizes the egg. A seed develops around the embryo. Hummingbirds and some types of bats also fertilize

The inside of this flower shows the male and female parts.

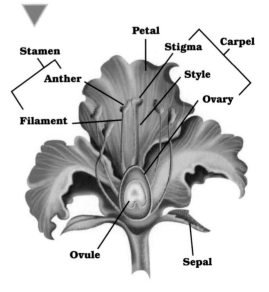

37

flowers while getting the benefit of sugary sap to drink.

What happened to the alternation of generations? The flowering plant is a sporophyte. The male gametophyte has become just a few specialized cells that produce the pollen and the pollen tube. The female gametophyte is also just a few cells that produce the egg and the embryo sac.

Monocots and Dicots

The seeds have been dispersed and have landed in a place where conditions are right. When seeds absorb water, and oxygen and sunlight are present, they germinate, or begin to grow. The first parts to emerge are called seed leaves, or cotyledons. Either one seed leaf emerges or a pair of them do. This difference creates the two main groups into which angiosperms are divided. Those with one seed leaf are monocotyledons, or monocots for short. Those with two seed leaves are dicotyledons, or dicots. Scientifically, monocots are usually placed in Class *Liliopsida* and dicots in Class *Magnoliopsida.*

Seed leaves usually bear little resemblance to the true leaves that will later appear on the growing plant. In the meantime, though, the cotyledons provide food for the growing plant.

Grasses are the most common monocots, though the huge orchid Family is also part of the Class. The one seed leaf is rarely visible, either remaining in the seed or in the ground. The leaves of monocots usually have veins arranged parallel to each other lengthwise. If you look at a blade of grass, you will see this arrangement.

The vascular bundles of a monocot are scattered loosely throughout the stem. In addition, flower parts such as petals and sepals occur in threes or multiples of three. The root system is primarily a single large taproot.

The two seed leaves of dicots are often visible above the ground. The veins are arranged in a net throughout the leaves. Within the stem, the vascular bundles of a dicot are arranged in a circle toward the outside. Flower parts are in fours and fives or multiples of those numbers. Finally, the root system is fibrous, with many small roots anchoring the plant in the ground.

Reaching for the Sun

Some plants have adapted in interesting ways to obtain the sunlight they need. In a field of grown sunflowers, all the flower heads point the same direction—toward

The major differences between monocots and dicots

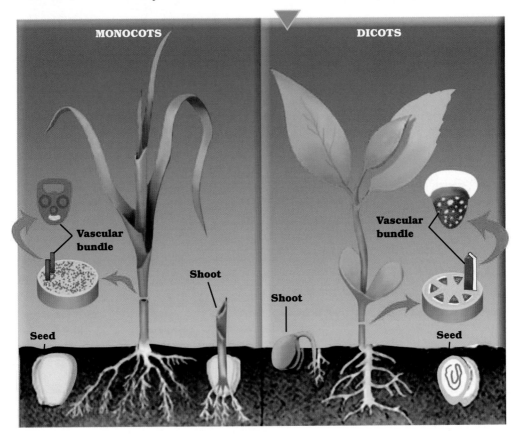

MONOCOTS **DICOTS**

Vascular bundle

Shoot

Seed

Vascular bundle

Shoot

Seed

Leaves That Eat

The low-growing marshland plant called the Venus flytrap has specialized lobed leaves that can trap small animals, especially insects. When such an animal brushes against sensitive hairs within the paired fleshy leaves, the trap quickly closes on the hinge connecting the leaves. Spikes on the outer edge of the lobed leaves prevent the animal from escaping. Digestive chemicals in the Venus flytrap digest the animal, absorbing minerals, such as nitrogen, that are missing in its nitrogen-poor marshy soil.

Venus fly-trap

Pitcher plant

Pitcher plants are also plants that "eat" insects. In this case, the ends of the leaves form tubular traps into which insects fall and from which they cannot escape. Sundews have leaves with sticky glands. After an unwary insect gets caught in the sticky substance, the leaf closes over it to digest it.

Sundew plant

the Sun. During the day, they turn on their stems in order to keep their heads facing the Sun. The flower head is clearly visible to insects that can aid in pollinating the plant. After the ovaries are pollinated, the Sun's warmth helps the seeds develop.

Some plants grow as vines. They climb tall trees so their leaves can reach the best sunlight. Vining plants start out with their roots in the ground. One of the most economically useful vines is rattan, a palm of Indonesia. The vines have been known to reach 500 feet (152 m) in length. The fast-growing vine is used to make furniture.

Some vines climb by using tendrils, which are small growths that are sensitive to touch. When they reach a support and touch it, the tendrils start to curl around the support.

Vines do not take food or drink from their support plant. Some plants, called parasites, do. They derive most, if not all, of their water and minerals from another plant. Mistletoe, for example, is a parasite that can grow on trees but not in soil. It sinks its roots into the host. Oddly enough, it still manufactures its own chlorophyll.

Other plants grow on trees but are not parasitic. These plants, called epiphytes, or air plants, just perch high up on trees. Epiphytes require a lot of sunlight, so they thrive way up in the forest canopy. They have roots, but the roots find nooks and crannies in the support, where they absorb whatever moisture is available there.

About half of all epiphytes belong to the orchid Family. Others are bromeliads which may have thick leaves that look like showy flowers, though the real flowers are different. The most famous bromelliad is the pineapple.

Careers

Plants are constantly being investigated by scientists who look for substances that might be useful in medicines. One of the first famous botanists was African American former slave George Washington Carver (1860–1943). He earned college degrees at Iowa State University and then taught at Tuskegee Institute in Alabama. He tried to find crops that could be a substitute for cotton. He eventually developed more than 325 products from peanuts.

Angiosperm Families

There are about 250 Families of dicots and about sixty Orders of monocots. Legumes belong to one of the most economically important Families. They include peas, beans, and clovers. There may be 17,000 Species in this Family.

The orchid Family is probably the largest Family of flowering plants, with perhaps 25,000 Species. Only a few are the big colorful flowers that people use as corsages. Many are small and grow in dense forests. Oddly, some orchids do not contain chlorophyll at all. Instead, they feed directly from the rotting material in the soil they live on. Such plants are called saprophytes.

The second largest Family of flowering plants is the daisy Family, *Asteraceae*. Also called composites, they may total 20,000 Species. A daisy flower head is not a single flower. Instead, it consists of hundreds of individual flowers.

The yellow center of a daisy flower head is made up of densely packed flowers called disk florets.

The Human Need for Variety

The differences among plants depend on the Species and where they grow. Not even all vegetables are alike, which is why we need to eat a variety of foods for health. Fruits and vegetables contain a lot of fiber, which is the cellulose of the vascular bundles. We do not digest cellulose, but it keeps our digestive systems functioning properly. Most fruits and vegetables contain nutrients that are good for our health. Some of them, people grow up knowing about— oranges for vitamin C and carrots for vitamin A.

People called nutritionists work with foods to make people healthier. They have recommended that grain foods, such as wheat, rice, and rye, be improved. For many years, grains were processed to remove the hull before being turned into white flour. Now,

Scientists experiment with plants.

nutritionists suggest we eat whole grains because they are better for us. In recent years, scientists have discovered all sorts of benefits from plants we did not know about before. A chemical called lutein in some vegetables is thought to prevent macular degeneration, a disease that can blind people. A chemical in soybeans might help prevent Alzheimer's disease. Plant chemicals are called phytochemicals and are opening up vast new areas of research.

43

Glossary

alternation of generations the formation of two different phases, usually one sexual and one asexual, during the reproduction of plants

anther the part of a flower stamen that produces and bears pollen

asexual reproduction the production of a new generation of a plant by means other than the union of a male and female, such as a spore or simple cell division

biome a major type of environment, which may be found in many places around the world, such as grasslands

carpel a female reproductive structure in a flower made up of the ovule, style, and stigma

cellulose the fibrous material made of glucose that forms the cell walls

chlorophyll the green material found in cells of most plants that is produced by photosynthesis

chromosomes thread-like collections of genes in the cell nucleus of most living things

cotyledons the first leaves of a seed plant, which contain the food for the plant to start growing; also called seed leaf

cuticle the outer protective layer of most surfaces of green plants, given off by the epidermis, or outer layer of cells

deciduous falling off, or shedding, especially of trees that lose their leaves each autumn

egg the female reproductive structure, or gamete; must be fertilized by a sperm in sexual reproduction

embryo the early stage of a plant after an egg has been fertilized but before the seed germinates

endosperm the starchy material in a seed that provides food for the growing embryo

epiphytes air plants, which get their nutrients and water from the air; usually grow perched on another plant

fertilized the result of a male and female gamete joining in sexual reproduction; also, the result of chemicals being added to soil to improve its nutrients

filament the stalk part of a stamen that supports the anther in a flower

gametes cells used in sexual reproduction that contains only half the chromosomes required for a new individual; two gametes—an egg and a sperm—must be joined to develop into a new organism

gametophyte in alternation of generations, the phase that produces cells, or gametes, containing only half the chromosomes needed for reproduction

genes units of inheritance, which together make up chromosomes

germinate to sprout, or begin to develop

glucose simple sugar; the cells of green plants produce it in photosynthesis and break it back down for energy

meiosis cell division in which the chromosomes do not duplicate first, so that each new cell contains only half the chromosomes needed in sexual reproduction

mitochondria the bodies within plant cells where glucose is burned for energy

mitosis simple cell division in which the chromosomes duplicate so that each new cell has a full set of chromosomes; carried out by all cells except reproductive cells

nutrient any chemical compound or element used to make a cell function or provide energy; food

ovary the enlarged base of the stigma that contains the ovule; it becomes the fruit

ovule the casing in which an embryo grows in a seed plant; it develops into the seed

petal a modified leaf in flower, often colored; together the petals make up the corolla

phloem the part of the vascular system of a higher plant that carries sugar and other nutrients to where they are needed; with xylem, makes up the vascular bundles

photosynthesis in green plants, the making of glucose from sunlight, carbon dioxide, and water in special parts of cells called chloroplasts; oxygen is given off in the process

pollen dust-like grains on the anther of flowering plants that may produce male cells when transferred to the female stigma

respiration the act of breathing; the process of exchanging gases in air

sepals modified leaves at the base of a flower; together they make up the calyx

sexual reproduction the production of a new generation of a plant by the union of a male and female part

sperm the male reproductive structure, or gamete; fertilizes the egg in sexual reproduction

spores reproductive bodies that develop into a new organism in asexual reproduction

sporophyte in alternation of generations, the phase that has cells containing all the chromosomes needed to develop into a new plant, which, in turn, forms spores

stamens the male reproductive structures in a flower made up of the filament and anther

stigma the end of the carpel of a flower on which pollen must be deposited for a seed to develop

stomata the openings in the surface of a plant that let in or keep out moisture and nutrients

style the stalk bearing a stigma above the ovary

taxonomy the science of classifying living things; a classification group is called a taxon

temperate a climate where the weather and temperatures are not extreme

transpiration in plants, the process of plants releasing water into the atmosphere

tropisms movements made by plants in response to outside sources, such as sunlight, water, or gravity

vascular having or being made up of veins that transport water and nutrients

whorls the parts of a plant that are arranged in small circles

xylem the part of the vascular system of a higher plant that transports sap up the stem, mainly in response to evaporation; with phloem, makes up the vascular bundles

For More Information

Books

DK Publishing. *Tree*. DK Eyewitness Books. DK Publishing, 2005

Dow, Lesley. *Incredible Plants*. Nature Company Discoveries Library. Time Life Books, 1997.

Musgrave, Toby, and Will Musgrave. *An Empire of Plants: People and Plants that Changed the World*. Cassell, 2003.

Fowler, Allan. *Plants That Eat Animals*. From Seed to Plant: Rookie Read-About Science (series). Children's Press, 2001.

From Bacteria to Plants. Science Explorer (series). Prentice Hall, 2000.

Web Sites

calphotos.berkeley.edu/flora
Surf a collection of more than 100,000 photos of plants and animals scientific name and common name.

www.ucmp.berkeley.edu/education/ explorations/tours/Trex/index.html
Study the relationships between living organisms.

www.ucmp.berkeley.edu/plants/ plantae.html
Explore the fossil records, life histories and ecology, systematics (classification), and morphology of organisms.

www.biology4kids.com
Check out the plant categories in this easy-to-use website

www.nmnh.si.edu/botany
Click on the links to learn more about the Smithsonian Institution's National Museum of Natural History botany section.

Publisher's note to educators and parents: Our editors have carefully reviewed these Web sites to ensure that they are suitable for children. Many Web sites change frequently, however, and we cannot guarantee that a site's future contents will continue to meet our high standards of quality and educational value. Be advised that children should be closely supervised whenever they access the Internet.

Index